ARCHEOLOGY
OF THE CIRCLE

BOOKS BY BRUCE WEIGL

POETRY

Executioner (1976)
A Sack Full of Old Quarrels (1977)
A Romance (1979)
The Monkey Wars (1985)
Song of Napalm (1988)
What Saves Us (1992)
Lies, Grace & Redemption (selected poems and an interview, edited by
    Harry Humes, 1995)
Sweet Lorain (1996)
Not on the Map (with Kevin Bowen, edited by John Deane, Dublin)

TRANSLATION

Poems from Captured Documents (translated from the Vietnamese
    with Thanh Nguyen, 1995)
Mountain River: Vietnamese Poetry From the Wars: 1945–1995
    (translated from the Vietnamese and edited with Nguyen Ba Chung
    and Kevin Bowen, 1998)
Angel Riding a Beast, poems by Liliana Ursu (translated with the
    author, 1998)

CRITICISM

The Giver of Morning: On Dave Smith (1993)
The Imagination as Glory: The Poetry of James Dickey (with T. R.
    Hummer, 1994)
Charles Simic: Essays on the Poetry (1996)

ANTHOLOGY

*Writing Between the Lines: An Anthology on War and Its Social
Consequences* (with Kevin Bowen, 1997)

ARCHEOLOGY OF THE CIRCLE

NEW AND SELECTED POEMS

Bruce
Weigl

Grove Press
New York

Published simultaneously in Canada
Printed in the United States of America

FIRST EDITION

Library of Congress Cataloging-in-Publication Data

Weigl, Bruce, 1949–
      Archeology of the circle : new and selected poems /
Bruce Weigl.
         p.   cm.
      ISBN 0-8021-3607-9
      I. Title.
      PS3573.E3835A89   1999
      811'.54–dc21   98-45237
                                                                   CIP

Design by Julie Duquet

Grove Press
841 Broadway
New York, NY 10003

99 00 01   10 9 8 7 6 5 4 3 2 1

For John Leeson, who read me a poem

CONTENTS

from *The Monkey Wars* (1985)

from *Song of Napalm* (1988)

ACKNOWLEDGMENTS

I gratefully acknowledge the generous support and vital encouragement of the editors who originally published the poems selected for this collection and the editors and publishers who published the books in which those poems were first gathered.

"Pigeons," "Mines," "Monkey," "Short," and "Anna Grasa" are reprinted from *Executioner* by Bruce Weigl. Copyright 1976, reprinted by permission of the Ironwood Press and with special thanks to Michael Cuddihy for his early and enabling support and in admiration of his brave spirit.

"Sailing to Dien Hua," "The Deer Hunter," "Convoy," and "Him, on the Bicycle" are reprinted from *A Sack Full of Old Quarrels* by Bruce Weigl. Copyright 1977, reprinted by permission of the Cleveland State University Poetry Center and with special thanks to Charles Simic and Alberta Turner for their care with this manuscript.

"A Romance," "On This Spot," "Cardinal," "The Man Who Made Me Love Him," "The Life Before Fear," "Dogs," "I Have Had My Time Rising and Singing," "Painting on a T'ang Dynasty Water Vessel," and "The Harp" are reprinted from *A Romance* by Bruce Weigl. Copyright 1979, reprinted by permission of the University of Pittsburgh Press and with special thanks to Paul Zimmer.

ment is made: "And We Came Home" in *American Poetry Review*, "The Singing and the Dancing," "Praise Wound Dirt Skin Sky," and "The Inexplicable Abandonment of Habit in Eclipse" in *Kenyon Review*, "Elegy for Her Whose Name You Don't Know" in *Harvard Review*, and "Our Independence Day" in *The Progressive*.

Many of these poems originally appeared in the following publications: *American Poetry Review, Antaeus, Black Warrior Review, Cimarron Review, Colorado Review, Field, Harper's, Harvard Review, Indiana Review, Ironwood, Kenyon Review, Manoa, Missouri Review, Mother Jones, New England Review, Ohio Review, Ploughshares, Poetry New York, Poetry Now, Prairie Schooner, Quarry West, Quarterly West, Southern Review, Tar River Poetry, Tendril, TriQuarterly, The New York Times, Western Humanities Review,* and *Willow Springs.*

I have been blessed with the generous and loving support of my family and of my teachers—Stuart Friebert, Thomas Lux, Charles Simic, Dave Smith and David Young—and of my longtime editor and friend Reginald Gibbons. I am grateful, too, for the support and patience of Morgan Entrekin, Ellen Levine, and Eric Price, without whom . . .

ARCHEOLOGY
OF THE CIRCLE

from
EXECUTIONER
(1 9 7 6)

PIGEONS

There's a man standing
in a coop,
his face is wet,
he says he's too old:
"You can't give them away
they just come back."
I follow him to the cellar.
Latin blessings on the wall,
sauerkraut in barrels,
he puts his arm around my waist
begins to make a noise,
pigeons bleeding.
We're both crying now
he moves his tongue around
pulls feathers from his coat.
A fantail he says,
the kind that hop around,
don't fly well.

MINES

1

In Vietnam I was always afraid of mines:
North Vietnamese mines, Vietcong mines,
American mines,
whole fields marked with warning signs.

A bouncing betty comes up waist high—
cuts you in half.
One man's legs were laid
alongside him in the Dustoff:
he asked for a chairback, morphine.
He screamed he wanted to give
his eyes away, his kidneys,
his heart . . .

2

You're taught to walk at night. Slowly, lift one leg,
clear the sides with your arms, clear the back,
front, put the leg down, like swimming.

MONKEY

1

I am you are he she it is
they are you are we are.
I am you are he she it is
they are you are we are.
When they ask for your number
pretend to be breathing.
Forget the stinking jungle,
force your fingers between the lines.
Learn to get out of the dew.
The snakes are thirsty.
Bladders, water, boil it, drink it.
Get out of your clothes:
You can't move in your green clothes.
Your O.D. in color issue clothes.
Get out the damp between your legs.
Get out the plates and those who ate.
Those who spent the night.
Those small Vietnamese soldiers.
They love to hold your hand.
A fine man is good to hard.

Back away from their dark cheeks.
Small Vietnamese soldiers.
They love to love you.
I have no idea how it happened,
I remember nothing but light.

2

I don't remember the hard
swallow of the lover.
I don't remember the burial
of ears.
I don't remember the time
of the explosion.
This is the place curses are
manufactured: delivered like
white tablets.
The survivor is spilling his bed pan.
He slips one in your pocket,
you're finally satisfied.
I don't remember the heat
in the hands,
the heat around the neck.
Good times bad times sleep
get up work. Sleep get up
good times bad times.
Work eat sleep good bad work times.

I like a certain cartoon of wounds.
The water which refuses to dry.
I like a little unaccustomed mercy.
Pulling the trigger is all we have.
I hear a child.

3

I dropped to the bottom of a well.
I have a knife.
I cut someone with it.
Oh, I have the petrified eyebrows
of my Vietnam monkey.
My monkey from Vietnam.
My monkey.
Put your hand here.
It makes no sense.
I beat the monkey with a sword.
I didn't know him.
He was bloody.
He lowered his intestines
to my shoes. My shoes
spit-shined the moment
I learned to tie the bow.
I'm not on speaking terms
with anyone. In the wrong climate
a person can spoil,
the way a pair of boots
slows you down . . .

I don't know when I'm sleeping.
I don't know if what I'm saying
is anything at all.
I'll lay on my monkey bones.

4

I'm tired of the rice falling
in slow motion like eggs from
the smallest animal.
I'm twenty-five years old,
quiet, tired of the same mistakes,
the same greed, the same past.
The same past with its bleat
and pound of the dead,
with its hand grenade tossed
into a hooch on a dull Sunday
because when a man dies like that
his eyes sparkle,
his nose fills with witless nuance
because a farmer in Bong Son
has dead cows lolling
in a field of claymores
because the vc tie hooks
to their comrades
because a spot of blood
is a number
because a woman
is lifting her dress across
the big pond . . .

If we're soldiers we should smoke them
if we have them. Someone's bound
to point us in the right direction
sooner or later.

I'm tired and I'm glad you asked.

5

There is a hill.
Men run top hill.
Men take hill.
Give hill to man.

*

Me and my monkey
and me and my monkey
my Vietnamese monkey
my little brown monkey
came with me
to Guam and Hawaii
in Ohio he saw
my people he
jumped on my daddy
he slipped into mother
he baptized my sister
he's my little brown monkey
he came here from heaven
to give me his spirit imagine
my monkey my beautiful
monkey he saved me lifted

me above the punji
sticks above the mines
above the ground burning
above the dead above
the living above the
wounded dying the wounded
dying above my own body
until I am me.

*

Men take hill away from smaller men.
Men take hill and give to fatter man.
Men take hill. Hill has number.
Men run up hill. Run down hill.

SHORT

There's a bar girl on Trung Hung Do who has half a ten piaster note I tore in my drunken relief to be leaving the country. She has half and I have half, if I can find it. If I lost it, it wasn't on purpose, it's all I have to remember her. She has a wet sheet, a PX fan, PX radio and half a ten piaster note, as if she cared to remember me. She thought it was stupid to tear money and when I handed it to her she turned to another soldier, new in country, who needed a girl. I hope I burn in hell.

ANNA GRASA

I came home from Vietnam.
My father had a sign
made at the foundry:
WELCOME HOME BRUCE
in orange glow paint.
He rented spotlights,
I had to squint.
WELCOME HOME BRUCE.

Out of the car I moved
up on the sign dreaming
myself full. The sign that cut the sky.
My eyes burned.

But behind the terrible thing
I saw my grandmother,
beautiful Anna Grasa.
I couldn't tell her tell her.

I clapped to myself,
clapped to the sound
of her dress.
I could've put it on
she held me so close,
both of us could be
inside.

from
A SACK FULL
OF OLD QUARRELS
(1977)

SAILING TO BIEN HOA

In my dream of the hydroplane I'm sailing to Bien Hoa. The shrapnel in my thighs like tiny glaciers. I remember a flower, a kite, a mannikin playing the guitar, a yellow fish eating a bird, a truck floating in urine, a rat carrying a banjo, a fool counting the cards, a monkey praying, a procession of whales and far off, two children eating rice, speaking French. I'm sure of the children, their damp flute, the long line of their vowels.

THE DEER HUNTER

for Jack Flowers

In late September
he starts to feel excited
so he hunts squirrels.

Some days are so warm
the ones shot in the morning
smell bad
by the time you leave the field.

It's good practice
"you have to stand downwind,
be quiet and watch the trees."

He can find a squirrel.
He can flip his fingernail
on the butt of his gun
make a noise like two or three
fox squirrels cutting on hickories

"and deer are just like squirrels
you just wait and when a buck walks by
you shoot him . . ."

CONVOY

On a convoy from Bong Son to Hue we stop at a Vietnamese graveyard. People set up shelter halves right over the top of gravestones: one rock wall just in case. It's raining. I smell people.

Two in the morning someone wakes me for guard. I'm out of bed, standing in the cold. The man next to me walks over to talk. A helicopter is parked thirty yards in front of us and in the moon it begins to move. My friend becomes leader, he wants to fire, I'm afraid of an explosion. He tells me to circle the ship while he covers.

At the window It's dark, no moon. Inside the pilot, restlessly turning in his sleep, rocking his ship.

HIM, ON THE BICYCLE

"There was no light; there was no light at all . . . "

In a liftship near Hue
the door gunner is in a trance.
He's that driver who falls
asleep at the wheel
between Pittsburgh and Cleveland
staring at the Ho Chi Minh Trail.

Flares fall,
where the river leaps
I go stiff
I have to think, tropical.

The door gunner sees movement,
the pilot makes small circles:
four men running carrying rifles,
one man on a bicycle
in the middle of the jungle.

He pulls me out of the ship
there's firing far away.
I'm on the back of the bike
holding his hips.

It's hard pumping for two,
I hop off the bike.

I'm brushing past trees,
the man on the bike stops pumping,
lifts his feet,
we don't waste a stroke.
His hat flies off,
I catch it behind my back,
put it one. I want to live forever.

Like a blaze
streaming down the trail.

from
A ROMANCE
(1979)

A ROMANCE

The skinny red-haired girl gets up
from the bar and dances
over to the jukebox
and punches the buttons as if
she were playing the piano—
below the white points of her pelvis
an enormous belt buckle
shaped like the head of a snake
with two red rhinestone eyes
which she polishes with the heels of her hands
making circles on her own fine thighs
and looking up
she catches me staring, my lust like a flag
waving at her across the room
as her big mean boyfriend
runs hillbilly after hillbilly off the table
in paycheck nine-ball games.

It is always like this with me in bars,
wanting women I know
I'll have to get my face
punched bloody to love.
Or she could be alone,
and I could be dull enough from liquor

to imagine my face interesting enough to take her
into conversation while I count my money
hoping to jesus I have enough
to get us both romantic.
I don't sleep anyway so I go to bars
and tell my giant lies to women
who have heard them from me,
from the thousands of me
out on the town with our impossible strategies
for no good reason but our selves,
who are holy.

ON THIS SPOT

This is where the old woman lifted her dress, pulled down her stiff underwear and pissed in the alley. I was standing in the dark cooling my heels. She didn't see me as she came through the door, squatted next to the bar owner's white El Dorado. I'm glad she didn't see me. I'm glad I watched her piss so hard her eyes closed. When she finished and wiped herself with the handkerchief and pulled the dress down around her thick ankles, I almost called to her.

CARDINAL

She is more beautiful than all her red husbands,
more indifferent toward the dry seeds on the window.
You don't notice by her color though the gray is perfect gray,
nor by her song though it cuts through you,
not even by the way she flits upward branch to branch,
female shape ascending inside the shuddering tree—
it's her head, the way she tilts it side to side,
pure movement, lifting when the wind catches
her small belly as she leans but doesn't let go.

THE MAN WHO MADE ME LOVE HIM

All I know about this man
is that he played the trumpet
from his bedroom window.
Evenings we could hear him
trying to play something
while we laughed at the din
and called him names.

I want to sing about this
but all I know
is that it was near dark
so I missed the way home
and stopped to rest in the churchyard
where gold carp lolled in the holy pond.

I was seven and the man who played the trumpet
took me to the roundhouse
where he said the hobos slept,
and though I knew the tracks
and the woods surrounding them,
I didn't know that secret.

He made me take him into my mouth,
my face rose and fell with his hips
and the sun cut through boxcars
waiting to be emptied.

THE LIFE BEFORE FEAR

When Acey O'Neil smacked his brother Herbert
on the side of his head with a two-by-four
I thought Herbert would die,
but he didn't even bleed,
he just lay there, dulled out some
and shook as though whipped with joy.
And then he got up.
He let us feel the lump on his head
not so much out of goodness,
as out of a need to be touched.
After we each had a turn
Herbert raised his face
and wandered off stiffly
like a man who hears his name
called across a great distance.

DOGS

I bought a bar girl in Saigon
cigarettes, watches, and Tide soap
to sell on the black market
and she gave me a room to sleep in
and all the cocaine I could live through
those nights I had to leave.
I would sometimes meet them, on the stairs,
and she would be wrapped in the soldier
who was always drunk, smiling,
her smell all over him.

She ran once to the room screaming
about dogs and pulled me down to the street
where a crowd of Vietnamese gathered
watching two stuck.
The owners fought about whose fault it was.
The owner of the male took off his sandal,
began to beat the female;
the owner of the female
kicked the male
but they did not part,
the beating made her tighten
and her tightening made him swell
as she dragged him down the street
the crowd running after them.

I remembered my grandfather,
how his pit bull locked up
the same way with the neighbor's dog.
The neighbor screamed and kicked
and the cop with his nightstick
sucked his teeth and circled
the dogs as the dogs circled.
Yet my grandfather knew what to do—
not cold water, warm,
warm and pour it slow.

I HAVE HAD MY TIME
RISING AND SINGING

When I was two I crawled out
onto the ruined landing
in the red apartment building
next to the Catholic church
where I would grow up mean and steal
quarters from the holy pond.
I was a late walker
and at two I still hugged the floor
as the dizzy man hugs the ground
after spinning too long in a dance.
At the time I'm sure it was fear
but now I'm grown and say it was
more that I wanted to *know* the ground before I gave it up,
and besides, I was a fast crawler
and could tear across the room before my sister
who walked early, who ran when I was born.
I don't remember why I was on the landing,
why I crawled away from my mother.
I don't even remember the fall—
but the hanging on as I fell
my fingernails filling with splinters,
and I remember the doctor,

and the two nurses, and my father
holding me down as they pulled the splinters out,
and I imagine my screaming,
how it must have come on its own,
how it must have lasted
until we were all pale, all sobbing
until I was lifted to the back seat of my father's car
my head cradled in my mother's hands until sleep
lulled me from the pain to the memory of pain.
This, I think, is what is wrong with me.
I think this is why I *run* down stairs
as if to outrun the falling I'm certain is near,
as if to outlive the darkness I know I must have seen,
as if to survive, as I once did,
on one more span of stairs,
beautifully disguised to myself
as a child.

PAINTING ON A T'ANG DYNASTY WATER VESSEL

Small girl leading a horse
its heavy lathered thighs steaming upward
dwarfing her at awkward angles
she is stopped
as if by some urgent recollection,
bundle of white flowers in her free hand.
Beyond her the moon before the willows
the boat of drunken fishermen and mountains,
green peaks on the neck,
on the farthest peak
two men trying to say good-bye,
one with a gift of thanks
the other gazing down the path
to his house lit by a single lamp
and his wife kneeling by the cooking
and his daughter leading a horse
its . . . no, I've come around,
this thing has turned completely around in my hands.
Someone must have meant this,
they painted it so
when you picked it up
hundreds of years later

you'd find the girl
waiting for her father
on the mountains past the loud willows
in the moon.

THE HARP

When he was my age and I was already a boy
my father made a machine in the garage.
A wired piece of steel
with many small and beautiful welds
ground so smooth they resembled rows of pearls.

He went broke with whatever it was.
He held it so carefully in his arms.
He carried it foundry to foundry.
I think it was his harp,
I think it was what he longed to make
with his hands for the world.

He moved it finally from the locked closet
to the bedroom
to the garage again
where he hung it on the wall
until I climbed and pulled it down
and rubbed it clean
and tried to make it work.

from
THE MONKEY WARS
(1985)

AMNESIA

If there was a world more disturbing than this
Where black clouds bowed down and swallowed you whole
And overgrown tropical plants
Rotted, effervescent in the muggy twilight and monkeys
Screamed something
That came to sound like words to each other
Across the triple-canopy jungle you shared,
You don't remember it.

You tell yourself no and cry a thousand days.
You imagine the crows calling autumn into place
Are your brothers and you could
If only the strength and will were there
Fly up to them to be black
And useful to the wind.

GIRL AT THE CHU LAI LAUNDRY

All this time I had forgotten.
My miserable platoon was moving out
One day in the war and I had my clothes in the laundry.
I ran the two dirt miles,
Convoy already forming behind me. I hit
The block of small hooches and saw her
Twist out the black rope of her hair in the sun.
She did not look up at me,
Not even when I called to her for my clothes.
She said I couldn't have them,
They were wet . . .

Who would've thought the world stops
Turning in the war, the tropical heat like hate
And your platoon moves out without you,
Your wet clothes piled
At the feet of the girl at the laundry,
Beautiful with her facts.

BURNING SHIT AT AN KHE

Into that pit
   I had to climb down
With a rake and matches; eventually,
   You had to do something
Because it just kept piling up
   And it wasn't our country, it wasn't
Our air thick with the sick smoke
   So another soldier and I
Lifted the shelter off its blocks
   To expose the homemade toilets:
Fifty-five-gallon drums cut in half
   With crude wood seats that splintered.
We soaked the piles in fuel oil
   And lit the stuff
And tried to keep the fire burning.
   To take my first turn
I paid some kid
   A care package of booze from home.
I'd walked past the burning once
   And gagged the whole heart of myself—
It smelled like the world
   Was on fire,
But when my turn came again
   There was no one

So I stuffed cotton up my nose
   And marched up that hill. We poured
And poured until it burned and black
   Smoke curdled
But the fire went out.
   Heavy artillery
Hammered the evening away in the distance,
   Vietnamese laundry women watched
From a safe place, laughing.
   I'd grunted out eight months
Of jungle and thought I had a grip on things
   But we flipped the coin and I lost
And climbed down into my fellow soldiers'
   Shit and began to sink and didn't stop
Until I was deep to my knees. Liftships
   Cut the air above me, the hacking
Blast of their blades
   Ripped dust in swirls so every time
I tried to light a match
   It died
And it all came down on me, the stink
   And the heat and the worthlessness
Until I slipped and climbed
   Out of that hole and ran

Past the olive drab
    Tents and trucks and clothes and everything
Green as far from the shit
    As the fading light allowed.
Only now I can't fly.
    I lay down in it
And finger paint the words of who I am
    Across my chest
Until I'm covered and there's only one smell,
    One word.

1955

After mass Father rinsed the chalice with wine
Again and again.
Drunk before noon
He'd sleep it off in the sacristy
While the other altar boys and I
Rummaged through the sacred things, feeling up
The blessed linen and silk vestments,
Swinging the censer above us so it whistled.
We put our hands on everything we could reach
Then woke the father for mass.

In summer the wool cassock itched
And I sweated through the white lace surplice.
My head reeled from incense
So I mumbled through the Latin prayers
And learned to balance the paten
Gracefully under their chins, my face
Turned away from the priest
Who dipped into the cup
As if to pluck a fish
And just like that something took me by the brain
And I saw myself
Torn loose from the congregation,

Floating like an impossible
Balloon of myself and I thought
This must be what my life is
Though I didn't know what it meant
And I couldn't move or swallow and thought I'd panic
Until father scowled and nudged me down the altar railing
To the next mouth
Open in the O of acceptance
So much like a scream
That can't get out of the lungs . . .
I don't know why my hands should shake,
I'm only remembering something.

SONG FOR THE LOST PRIVATE

The night we were to meet in the hotel
In the forbidden Cholon district
You didn't show
So I drank myself into a filthy room with a bar girl
Who had terrible scars
She ran her fingers over
As we bartered for the night.
Drunk I couldn't do anything, angry
I threw the mattress to the street
And stood out on the balcony naked,
Cursing your name to the night.
She thought I was crazy,
She tried to give my money back.
I don't know how to say I tried again.
I saw myself in the mirror and couldn't move.
In her fist she crushed the paper money,
She curled in sleep away from me
So I felt cruel, cold, and small arms fire
Cracked in the marketplace below.
I thought I heard you call back my name then
But white flares lit the sky
Casting empty streets in clean light
And the firing stopped.

I couldn't sleep so I touched her
Small shoulders, traced the curve of her spine,
Traced the scars, the miles
We were all from home.

KILLING CHICKENS

Never mind what you think.
The old man did not rush
Recklessly into the coop the last minute.
The chickens hardly stirred
For the easy way he sang to them.
Red sun is burning out
Past slag heaps of the mill. The old man
Touches the blade of his killing knife
With his fat thumb.
I'm in the backyard on a quilt
Spread out under the heavy dark plums
He cooks for his whiskey.
He walks among the hens singing
His chicken song way down in his throat
Until he finds the one who's ready
And he holds her to his barrel chest.

What did you think?
Did you think you just jerk the bird
From her roost and hack her head off?

Beyond the coop
I see the fleeting white dress of my grandmother
As she crosses and recrosses the porch
To fill the bucket with scalding water.

How easy the feathers will come
When she drowns them for plucking
And clouds the air with a stench
I can't stand not to breathe.
I'm not even a boy yet but I watch
The old man sing out into the yard,
His knife already at the chicken's throat
When everything begins to spin in my world–
He slices off the head without a squawk,
And swirls the bird in circles, a fine
Blood spray fanning out far enough
To reach me where I wait
Obediently, where I can't stop watching
The head the old man picks up,
His free hand becomes a puppet chicken
Clucking at me, pecking my head with the cold beak
Until I cry for him to stop,
Until he pins me down, clucking, laughing, blood
All over his hands.

He did it so I would remember him
I tell myself all these years later.
He did it because it was his last summer
Among us. In August he didn't feel the fly
Come into his cancerous ear and lay its eggs.

He didn't feel the maggots hatch
As he sat dazed with pills in the sun.
He pecked my head and laughed out of love,
Out of love he snatched me roughly to his chest
And sang his foreign songs way,
Way down in his throat.

THE LAST LIE

Some guy in the miserable convoy
Raised up in the back of our open truck
And threw a can of c-rations at a child
Who called into the rumble for food.
He didn't toss the can, he wound up and hung it
On the child's forehead and she was stunned
Backwards into the dust of our trucks.

Across the sudden angle of the road's curving
I could still see her when she rose
Waving one hand across her swollen, bleeding head,
Wildly swinging her other hand
At the children who mobbed her,
Who tried to take her food.

I grit my teeth to myself to remember that girl
Smiling as she fought off her brothers and sisters.
She laughed
As if she thought it were a joke
And the guy with me laughed
And fingered the edge of another can
Like it was the seam of a baseball
Until his rage ripped
Again into the faces of children
Who called to us for food.

TEMPLE NEAR QUANG TRI, NOT ON THE MAP

Dusk, the ivy thick with sparrows
Squawking for more room
Is all we hear; we see
Birds move on the walls of the temple
Shaping their calligraphy of wings.
Ivy is thick in the grottos,
On the moon-watching platform
And ivy keeps the door from fully closing.

The point man leads us and we are
Inside, lifting
The white washbowl, the smaller bowl
For rice, the stone lanterns
And carved stone heads that open
Above the carved faces for incense.
But even the bamboo sleeping mat
Rolled in the corner,
Even the place of prayer is clean.
And a small man

Sits legs askew in the shadow
The farthest wall casts
Halfway across the room.

He is bent over, his head
Rests on the floor and he is speaking something
As though to us and not to us.
The CO wants to ignore him;
He locks and loads and fires a clip into the walls
Which are not packed with rice this time
And tells us to move out.

But one of us moves toward the man,
Curious about what he is saying.
We bend him to sit straight
And when he's nearly peaked
At the top of his slow uncurling
His face becomes visible, his eyes
Roll down to the charge
Wired between his teeth and the floor.
The sparrows
Burst off the walls into the jungle.

SURROUNDING BLUES ON
THE WAY DOWN

I was barely in country.
We slipped under rain black clouds
Opening around us like orchids.
He'd come to take me into the jungle
So l felt the loneliness
Though I did not yet hate the beautiful war.
Eighteen years old and a man
Was telling me how to stay alive
In the tropics he said would rot me—

Brothers of the heart he said and smiled
Until we came upon a mama san
Bent over from her stuffed sack of flowers.
We flew past her but he hit the brakes hard,
He spun the tires backwards in the mud.
He did not hate the war either,
Other reasons made him cry out to her
So she stopped,
She smiled her beetle-black teeth at us.
In the air she raised her arms.

I have no excuse for myself.
I sat in that man's jeep in the rain
And watched him slam her to her knees,
The plastic butt of his M-16
Crashing down on her.
I was barely in country, the clouds
Hung like huge flowers, black
Like her teeth.

ELEGY FOR A.

Four years since the morning you leaped
Out from under the waves of pain
Into which you had to awake
One day in the middle of your life.
I think of you
Nights my own confusion
Runs away with itself,
Darting in and out of the dark
Possibilities like a spirit.
I don't know if I can speak to you,
I don't know why we long so for the dead
Who can do us no good, eventually,
Like you, a flood of stars will drown us all.

You jumped because at three A.M.
You passed the open balcony door
And for the hundredth night you couldn't sleep.
That day in your bed I'd tried to hold you,
To drag you back to us
But I didn't understand the way you
Floundered with your arms,
The way you gulped for air.
Inside you something was shaking out of control,
Something was wrong.

Four years already.
I wanted to tell you that my son
Who bears your name into the world
Is strong and sure of himself;
That your wife has found someone else, someone
Remarkably like you
In your gentle time,
And that sometimes, friend, I close my eyes
To see you descend on the wings of your bathrobe
Speaking, I imagine, some warning in the instant it took
Before you smashed away
The hold the dark had on you.

NOISE

Next door the newlyweds
Scream at each other, three A.M.
I hate your fucking guts he says
Through the open summer window
To the sky crowded with stars.
Freight trains at the roundhouse
Shake the windows, shake the house.
Just please get out she says
And someone throws something
Glass against the wall.
This is none of my business
But they've waked me with their noise.
The clots of stars or the full moon
Could be behind this because I feel the same
Anger and the trains make so much noise tonight.

Everyone lies and cheats and says hateful things.
The newlyweds next door
Spit the words out at each other.
From room to room I see them move
In their underwear, the windows
Open, she is lovely, she is
Wringing her hands
And he is pacing in another room then disappears

And she is standing by the window, crying,
The trains so loud tonight
And the trainmen shout the couplings into place—
A triangle of nervous noise
Because the noise is in my head too,
The noise is always in my head.

REGRET FOR THE MOURNING DOVES
WHO FAILED TO MATE

I passed the window and saw their lovely flash of wings
In the ivy all tangled and fluttering.
Something about gravity is deeply important
To whether or not it works for them
And gravity keeps these two from mating.
Even in the rain he tried
His small dance up her back
As she clung to the ivy
Easing the angle for him.
But I'm sorry,

I'm here to say they didn't make it.
Their nest stays empty
And the wind eats it up bit by bit
The way they constructed it together—
Some twigs, some brown grass woven,
A bit of color from a scrap of paper
Returned to litter the street.
And the winter keeps us locked indoors
Where we peck at each other,
Our voices thin and cold
Saying always what we don't mean,
Our hearts all future,
Our love nearly gone.

MERCY

Enough snow over last night's ice
So the road appears safe, appears
As a long white scar unfolding.
Ohio, cold hawk off Lake Erie,
And only enough light to see vague outlines:
The castlelike shape of mill stacks
And the shape of gulls' wings
Dipping to the parking lot for garbage
Lashed this way and that by the wind
These nights have in common.
I pumped gas from five to midnight
For minimum wage
Because I had a family and the war
Made me stupid, and only dead enough
To clean windshields.
When you clean the windshields of others
You see your own face
Reflected in the glass.
I looked and saw only enough hope
To lift me car to car and in between
I breathed the oil smell and the fly strips
And the vending candy air.

The *Gulf* sign clanged in the gale,
The plate glass strained like a voice
I thought would shatter
Yet still cars arrived, dim headlights
Casting the snow into a silver sheet,
Then the fenders like low clouds,
Then the bundled families
And the hushed sound
When father opens the window
And slips me the money for gas.
Only a second when our eyes catch
And the wind shows some mercy.

SMALL SONG FOR ANDREW

My baby boy cries and cries and cries
So we feed him and love him
And walk into the cool autumn night
Traffic streaking past
We play music for him
Dance him around the house
Pull out bowls and lids and spoons
Dial the phone so he can hear
Love long distance
Ride him in the stroller
Kiss his face and neck and feet
We rock him
We sing to him
Until finally he sleeps
So deeply he hangs his head
Backwards into my arms
So I carry him into his warm room
And its jungle of our indulgences
And he is more beautiful
Than the light
Before the light has touched anything

THE STREETS

On this day in this year of strangeness
The starlings may or may not
Come and I stay too long at the window
Waiting for the oily rainbow wings,
For the feet that are crosses in the snow.
In this long rift of speechlessness
I fall away from my life
And the cold careless winter. Fall

Through dark space to surface
In the river where we swam as children,
My arms treading water, rippling circles,
The locust clacking,
All the days of a life left,
All the hate buried deep another season.

Yet what I love is close at hand:
Wind cutting through the city
Street after mad street;
Circle of starlings when they come
Like blossoms in the waking landscape of a city
Where the gentle die,
Where the bad go on pounding the air.

SNOWY EGRET

My neighbor's boy has lifted his father's shotgun and stolen
Down to the backwaters of the Elizabeth
And in the moon he's blasted a snowy egret
From the shallows it stalked for small fish.

Midnight. My wife wakes me. He's in the backyard
With a shovel so I go down half-drunk with pills
That let me sleep to see what I can see and if it's safe.
The boy doesn't hear me come across the dewy grass.
He says through tears he has to bury it,
He says his father will kill him
And he digs until the hole is deep enough and gathers
The egret carefully into his arms
As if not to harm the blood-splattered wings
Gleaming in the flashlight beam.

His man's muscled shoulders
Shake with the weight of what he can't set right no matter what,
But one last time he tries to stay a child, sobbing
Please don't tell . . .
He says he only meant to flush it from the shadows,
He only meant to watch it fly
But the shot spread too far

Ripping into the white wings
Spanned awkwardly for a moment
Until it glided into brackish death.

I want to grab his shoulders,
Shake the lies loose from his lips but he hurts enough,
He burns with shame for what he's done,
With fear for his hard father's
Fists I've seen crash down on him for so much less.
I don't know what to do but hold him.
If I let go he'll fly to pieces before me.
What a time we share, that can make a good boy steal away,
Wiping out from the blue face of the pond
What he hadn't even known he loved, blasting
Such beauty into nothing.

SONG OF NAPALM

for my wife

After the storm, after the rain stopped pounding,
We stood in the doorway watching horses
Walk off lazily across the pasture's hill.
We stared through the black screen,
Our vision altered by the distance
So I thought I saw a mist
Kicked up around their hooves when they faded
Like cut-out horses
Away from us.
The grass was never more blue in that light, more
Scarlet; beyond the pasture
Trees scraped their voices into the wind, branches
Crisscrossed the sky like barbed wire
But you said they were only branches.

Okay. The storm stopped pounding.
I am trying to say this straight: for once
I was sane enough to pause and breathe
Outside my wild plans and after the hard rain
I turned my back on the old curses. I believed
They swung finally away from me . . .

But still the branches are wire
And thunder is the pounding mortar,
Still I close my eyes and see the girl
Running from her village, napalm
Stuck to her dress like jelly,
Her hands reaching for the no one
Who waits in waves of heat before her.

So I can keep on living,
So I can stay here beside you,
I try to imagine she runs down the road and wings
Beat inside her until she rises
Above the stinking jungle and her pain
Eases, and your pain, and mine.

But the lie swings back again.
The lie works only as long as it takes to speak
And the girl runs only as far
As the napalm allows
Until her burning tendons and crackling
Muscles draw her up
Into that final position

Burning bodies so perfectly assume. Nothing
Can change that; she is burned behind my eyes
And not your good love and not the rain-swept air
And not the jungle green
Pasture unfolding before us can deny it.

from
SONG OF NAPALM
(1 9 8 8)

INTRODUCTION

Wars are meant to be forgotten, the Vietnam War like any other. Memory resists them. Their reality bleeds away, surviving in fragments. The fragments are elusive, drifting apart. The mist that covers Dak To this morning covers them. They are enfolded in their own darkness.

Sometimes a single recollected moment lights up the sky of memory and brings it all back. The mind's eye fills with broken sunlight and soiled rain. Pieces of time assemble, counting off, strung along the pulse, in breaths, in heartbeats. It's all burned in; the dream's inseparable from the dreamer.

Song of Napalm is poetry performed in defiance of physical and moral death. It is compounded of explosive moments that illuminate a terrifying landscape, that lead us into the fire and out under the swollen black sky. Its incantatory power confronts us with that sense, particular to war, of things going utterly out of control, of all promises and sane assumptions being subsumed in limitless violence. The poet compels our complicity as his witnesses. Every line carries his distinctive voice; his special sensibility is such a constant presence that he seems to suffer and laugh unsoundly and be amazed right there beside us as we read his impacted, precise verse. He pursues every act and image to its essence, displays it for us and shakes it for meaning, strips it and puts it together again. His starkest lines are full of vitality and the energy of observation. Each captured fraction of experience is subjected to relentless scrutiny. Again and again, he brings us to the outer limits of our reference point, to that dread zone of the spirit where wars are fought and survived.

Bruce Weigl's poetry is a refusal to forget. It is an angry assertion of the youth and life that was spent in Vietnam with such vast prodigality, as though youth and life were infinite. Through his honesty and tough-mindedness, he undertakes the traditional duty of the poet: in the face of randomness and terror to subject things themselves to the power of art and thus bring them within the compass of moral comprehension.

—Robert Stone

THE WAY OF TET

Year of the monkey, year of the human wave,
the people smuggled weapons in caskets through the city
in long processions undisturbed
and buried them in Saigon graveyards.
At the feet of their small Buddhas
weary bar girls burned incense
before the boy soldiers arrived
to buy them tea and touch them
where they pleased. Twenty years
and the feel of a girl's body
so young there's no hair
is like a dream, but living is a darker thing,
the iron burning bee who drains the honey,
and he remembers her
twisting in what evening
light broke into the small room in the shack
in the labyrinth of shacks
in the alley where the lost and corrupted kept house.
He undressed her for the last time,
each piece of clothing
a sacrifice she surrendered to the war
the way the world had become.
Tomorrow blood would run in every province.

Tomorrow people would rise from tunnels everywhere
and resurrect something ancient from inside them,
and the boy who came ten thousand miles to touch her
small self lies beside the girl whose words he can't understand,
their song a veil between them.

She is a white bird in the bamboo, fluttering.
She is so small he imagines
he could hold all of her
in his hands and lift her to the black
sky beyond the illumination round's white light
where she would fly from her life
and the wounds from the lovers would heal,
the broken skin grow back.
But he need only touch her, only
lift the blanket from her shoulders
and the automatic shape of love unfolds,
the flare's light burning down on them,
lost in a wave that arrives
after a thousand years of grief
at their hearts.

SOME THOUGHTS ON THE
AMBASSADOR: BONG SON, 1967

Bunker the ambassador.

Does Mr. Bunker have a bunker?

He must have a bunker
with chrome faucets and a sauna
and a mama san to ease his mind.

They must call it
Mr. Bunker's bunker.

He must be shaking his head.

LZ NOWHERE

Nights I spent on the dusty runway
under the green liftship

tethered down from the wind of the highlands
shaping the moonlit fields

surrounding us like care.
I stroked the length of the blades

those nights
and moved the rudder and flaps

so it felt like legs parting
or someone's arms opening to me.

BREAKDOWN

With sleep that is barely under the surface
it begins, a twisting sleep as if a wire
were inside you and tried at night
to straighten your body.
Or it's like a twitch
through your nerves as you sleep
so you tear the sheet from the bed
to try to stop the pounding spine.
A lousy, worthless
sleep of strangers with guns,
children trapped in the alley,
the teenage soldiers glancing back
over their shoulders
the moment before
they squeeze the trigger.

I am going to stay here as long as I can.
I am going to sit in the garden as if nothing has happened
and let the bruised azaleas have their way.

ON THE ANNIVERSARY OF HER GRACE

Rain and low clouds blown through the valley,
rain down the coast raising the brackish
rivers at their high tides too high,
rain and black skies that come for you.

Not excellent and fair,
I wake from a restless night of dreams of her
whom I will never have again
as surely as each minute passing
makes impossible another small fulfillment
until there's only a lingering
I remember, a kiss I had imagined
would come again and again to my face.

Inside me the war had eaten a hole.
I could not touch anyone.
The wind blew through me to the green place
where they still fell in their blood.
I could hear their voices at night.
I could not undress in the light
her body cast in the dark rented room.

I could keep the dragons at the gate.
I could paint my face and hide
as shadow in the triple-canopy jungle.
I could not eat or sleep then walk all day
and all night watch a moonlit path for movement.

I could draw leeches from my skin
with the tip of a lit cigarette
and dig a hole deep enough to save me
before the sun bloodied the hills we could not take
even with our lives
but I could not open my arms to her
that first night of forgiveness.
I could not touch anyone.
I thought my body would catch fire.

APPARITION OF THE EXILE

There was another life of cool summer mornings, the dogwood
air and the slag stink so gray like our monsoon which we loved
for the rain and cool wind until the rot came into us. And I
remember the boys we were the evening of our departure, our
mothers waving through the train's black pluming exhaust; they
were not proud in their tears of our leaving, so don't tell me to
shut up about the war or I might pull something from my head,
from my head, from my head that you wouldn't want to see and
whoever the people are might be offended.

From the green country you reconstruct in your brain, from the
rubble and stink of your occupation, there is no moving out. A
sweet boy who got drunk and brave on our long ride into the
State draws a maze every day on white paper, precisely in his
room of years as if you could walk into it. All day he draws and
imagines his platoon will return from the burning river where
he sent them sixteen years ago into fire. He can't stop seeing the
line of trees explode in white phosphorous blossoms and the
liftship sent for them spinning uncontrollably beyond hope into
the Citadel wall. Only his mother comes these days, drying the
fruit in her apron **or singing** the cup of hot tea into his fingers
which, like barbed wire, web the air.

THE SOLDIER'S BRIEF EPISTLE

You think you're better than me,
cleaner or more good

because I did what you may have only
imagined as you leaned over the crib

or watched your woman sleep.
You think you're far away from me

but you're right here in my pants
and I can grab your throat

like a cock and squeeze.
And you want to know what it's like

before I go. It's like
a bad habit, pulling the trigger,

like a dream come true.
And he did not hide well enough

I would tell his family
in a language they do not understand,

but he did not cry out,
and he was very difficult to kill.

DIALECTICAL MATERIALISM

Through dark tenements and fallen temples
we wander into Old Hanoi,
oil lamps glowing in small
storefronts and restaurants
where those, so long ago my enemy,
sit on low chairs and praise the simple evening.
On one block
the rich steam from pho,
their morning and evening soup, rises,
on another
brown smoked ducks are strung up in a row.
The people talk and smoke,
men hold each other's hands again in that old way
and children,
their black and white laughter all around us,
kick the weighted feather
with such grace into the air
because the bombs have stopped. And further

to the Long Bien bridge
where we meet a man
filling buckets
hung across his back's yoke
to bring cool water to his corn
in the moonlight.

When we ask our questions
he points to a stone and stick
house beyond the dikes
one thousand meters from the bridge
our great planes
could not finally knock down.
He doesn't say
how he must have huddled
those nights with his family,
how he must have spread himself
over them
until the village bell
called them back to their beds.
There are questions which
people who have everything
ask people who have nothing
and they do not understand.

Hanoi, 1985

THE KISS

All the good-byes said and done
I climbed into the plane and sat down.
From the cold I was shaking and ached
to be away from the love
of those waving through the frozen window . . .

(Once as a boy I was lost in a storm,
funnel cloud twisting so near
I was pitched from my bicycle
into the ditch,
picked up by the wind and yellow sky,
my arms before me
feeling my way through the wind
I could not cry above.
Out of that black air of debris,
out of nowhere, my father bent down,
lifted me and ran
to the house of strangers.)

And again that day on the plane
he appeared to me,
my forgotten orders in his hands.

He bent down to put the envelope into my hand,
on my lips he kissed me hard
and without a word he was gone
into the cold again.
Through the jungle, through the highlands,
through all that green dying
I touched my fingers to my lips.

ELEGY

Into sunlight they marched,
into dog day, into no saints day,
and were cut down.
They marched without knowing
how the air would be sucked from their lungs,
how their lungs would collapse,
how the world would twist itself, would
bend into the cruel angles.

Into the black understanding they marched
until the angels came
calling their names,
until they rose, one by one from the blood.
The light blasted down on them.
The bullets sliced through the razor grass
so there was not even time to speak.
The words would not let themselves be spoken.
Some of them died.
Some of them were not allowed to.

from
WHAT SAVES US
(1 9 9 2)

HER LIFE RUNS LIKE A
RED SILK FLAG

Because this evening Miss Hoang Yen
sat down with me in the small
tiled room of her family house
I am unable to sleep.
We shared a glass of cold and sweet water.
On a blue plate her mother brought us
cake and smiled her betel-black teeth at me
but I did not feel strange in the house
my country had tried to bomb into dust.
In English thick and dazed as blood
she told me how she watched our planes
cross her childhood's sky,
all the children of Hanoi
carried in darkness to mountain hamlets, Nixon's
Christmas bombing. She let me hold her hand,
her shy unmoving fingers, and told me
how afraid she was those days and how this fear
had dug inside her like a worm and lives
inside her still, won't die or go away.
And because she's stronger, she comforted me,
said I'm not to blame,
the million sorrows alive in her gaze.
With the dead we share no common rooms.

With the frightened we can't think straight;
no words can bring the burning city back.
Outside on Hung Dao Street
I tried to say good-bye and held her hand
too long so she looked back through traffic
towards her house and with her eyes
she told me I should leave.
All night I ached for her and for myself
and nothing I could think or pray
would make it stop. Some birds sang morning
home across the lake. In small reed boats
the lotus gatherers sailed out
among their resuming white blossoms.

Hanoi, 1990

WHY NOTHING CHANGES
FOR MISS NGO THI THANH

December in Hanoi
is gray and wet and cold
but in the still dark morning
after tea and rice
she rides her bike through
waking streets, past fallen
temples, to the grim offices
of the War Crimes Commission
where she sorts through pictures
that tell a wordless, armless
story of their own.
But in her mind there are suspicions
and she imagines rooms
with great light in them,
she imagines time enough
to drift away, back
to the Perfume river and her lost
boy's heart. But grinding along
beneath her feet is a country,
a turtle on which her world
is balanced, and over space
vast as these lost lives
she must move with such care

it is all she can do to keep
from falling into the night
these dead inhabit
because they can't go home.
And against winter, against
history, she puts a little lipstick on,
some rouge, she ties a colored
scarf around her black hair.

Hanoi, 1985

THE LOOP

Blue unwelcome jays barge through trees in the flyway,
God of the great nothing hovering over us.
So long I've wanted the woman of the green year,
in my thighs and in my gut, evening sheen of sweat

on her body on the borrowed bed, summer tearing
apart from the inside, I rolled her nipple
between my lips like a bullet and from a bad
and green dream I was delivered to her forgiving hips.

But certain spirits still inhabit me.
Certain strangers have in their eyes a river on which
you may sail back to the killing ground. I fell back
into her eyes, her body like smoke, the cords of light

that connect us to the world pulsing and
cracking. Some boys fell before me in heaps, their arms
and legs flailing ridiculously through the smoke
and flash. I remember that. I remember

the smell of the Vietnamese woman's hair
on the crowded train as we slowed for the last curve
before home. I remember a necklace of human ears,
everything, in sunlight, I can't stop seeing.

WHAT SAVES US

We are wrapped around each other
in the back of my father's car parked
in the empty lot of the high school
of our failures, sweat on her neck
like oil. The next morning I would leave
for the war and I thought I had something
coming for that, I thought to myself
that I would not die never having
been inside her body. I lifted
her skirt above her waist like an umbrella
blown inside out by the storm. I pulled
her cotton panties up as high
as she could stand. I was on fire. Heaven
was in sight. We were drowning
on our tongues and I tried
to tear my pants off when she stopped
so suddenly we were surrounded
only by my shuddering
and by the school bells
grinding in the empty halls.

She reached to find something,
a silver crucifix on a silver chain,
the tiny savior's head
hanging, and stakes through his hands and his feet.
She put it around my neck and held me
so long my heart's black wings were calmed.
We are not always right
about what we think will save us.
I thought that dragging the angel down that night
would save me, but I carried the crucifix in my pocket
and rubbed it on my face and lips
nights the rockets roared in.
People die sometimes so near you,
you feel them struggling to cross over,
the deep untangling, of one body from another.

IN THE HOUSE OF IMMIGRANTS

After milk, the kittens spill out of their box,
weary mother cat snapping at them,
too young for so many babies. In the bedroom
the boy bows his cello painfully
down the hall, Mozart. He loves his practice
more than ball with the boys who call him
through the summer's open window. The grandfather
smokes, reads his Hungarian newspaper
moving his lips. The mother cooks
some nice chicken with garlic, some boiled
potatoes, and our children run in and out
of the house as if there were not enough time
to live because there isn't, the solstice sun
already gone below the oaks looming over us,
and I argue with the father.

                    He loves our country
no matter what, he says. There must
be sacrifices, our voices beginning to rise
above the cello, above the children,
above the kitchen noise until everyone freezes,
stares at us fearfully and with disappointment.

We've come too far to stop. I'm not
interested in details he says, only
the principle is important, his hands shaking
between us and a wronged light cast down
on his face until the mother steps
from the kitchen and tells us with her eyes to stop.
She shakes her finger at her husband and says
his name, stressing the syllables the way a mother
calls her child home across the dark
neighborhood and then she turns to me.
I was only a child she says.
They lined you up without a word
and shot you like a dog.
I won't listen to Russian music.
I don't care if you say it is beautiful.
I won't read Russian books.
I don't care what you say.
They buried people in the school yard where I played.

TEMPTATION

Either in the hotel D'Lido in Managua,
that faddish fifties bar in the garden
and all the hot water the people could not have
splashing extravagantly down your body
into the painted tile drain; or in
the bathhouse in Masaya, anonymous
artillery booming dully in the distance,
and the manliness, at the same time,
let down and untangled like hair,
all of us wrapped like mummies in towels,
speaking a simple Spanish to each other
through the heavy air, our faces visible
only vaguely through the steam. Or in Hanoi,
Christmas eighty-five, Russians
mill around the lobby,
dreaming their warm water port,
their eager interpreters
covering their mouths when they laugh,
and among them, the woman in the flowered *ao dais*
who called to you across the room with her eyes,
across the impossibility
as if imagining your white skin. Or in a cool
bed in Tay Ninh, where you slept with men
across the sheet's white field
through the burning afternoon,

the narrow highway of red dust,
the war-wasted plantations behind you
as you tried to match your breath with theirs
as if to bring them close. Or Lord,
in a dark unthinkable room in Bangkok
where in fever you dreamed that a bad cell,
a swirling red planet out of control
tried to kill the other holy cells
and take your body,
someone's lonely buddha
praying through an open window,
across the alley, across the marketplace,
waves of prayer.

SHELTER

I need cover tonight.
I need shelter from the wings
who beat my head into memory
where my sister sleeps
in the small upstairs bedroom
among the crucifixes and dried palm leaves,
among the lavender smell
of our grandmother's Sunday black silk dress
in her house where we've come as a family
after church,
the brothers from Belgrade
and the wives from across the river
which is called the river of blood.

In the crowded kitchen,
below my sleeping sister,
a beautiful dandelion salad
waits like a bouquet
with blood sausage on a plate
and black bread and dark wine,
and the aunts and uncles
and their children in their orbits,
and the language thick on my tongue
when I try to say the words
because the air is suddenly wronged.

My grandfather swears too loud.
His brothers only laugh.
The women shush them all, Eat,
eat they say across the room
but something's cut too deep this time
so the children are pushed
with grace towards the porch and backyard,
and from behind the tree
of drunken plums
I watch my grandfather
wave his pistol in the air
and his brothers reach for it
and the shot explode
through the low ceiling
and the bedroom floor
where my sister sleeps
and lives on.
I need shelter tonight.
I need the sleeping hands
to waken once again.

THEY NAME HEAVEN

I saw the moon over Plaza España
but it's not my moon
because of what this pale one has seen
pass in dark cells at the hands
of crazy rich men,
murder on their lips like salt.
Not the moon my little boy will see tonight
safe in the place of the great Republic,
near enough his mother
so he may find her even in his sleep.
Not the clean moon he calls to,
this one rises over Cuesta del Plomo
where the bones have already grown
back into the earth
until there is nothing
but the disappeared.
The moon who will no longer
let us understand each other.
How in darkness they came for you.
How in moonlight you passed through the city,
your hands bound,
your shirt ripped over your face.

How you must have known you would die
only wondered how long it would take,
what parts of the body they would relish
with their sticks and long knives,
those who make pacts under the moon,
who wash the blood away with rum,
and return to their sleeping families
to lift the acquiescent
nightgowns of their wives,
their drunken lips
fumbling upwards, always
upwards to the moon of flesh
they name heaven.

ON THE DICTATORSHIP
OF THE PROLETARIAT

At a party of the young Sandinistas in Managua,
neighborhood where the Somocistas had lived
and idled their long cars,
all the pretty people dance the salsa
and toast the liberation with fine rum.

Two winding miles down the hill
a barrio of tin-roofed shacks
spreads itself out like a sickness.
On dirt floors the people keep house,
they fetch their water in buckets,

through a field of garbage they pick like gulls
for a slice of fruit or scrap of meat.
A boy had grabbed my hand down there
and led me through the mud and morning
light, proud about something he wanted me to see,

a sewer being dug but now abandoned.
He jumped down into that ordinary hole
and waved his arms
like it was his grave he'd just defeated,
or like it was a monument,
because not having to shit
in the tall grass means something.

THE SKY IN DADUZA TOWNSHIP

Like a green turtle on the dusty highway
a small car is on its back, only burning,
black smoke curdling in plumes,
in great billows against the white sky
that opens itself to some terror.
A man calls to someone out of frame.
He cradles the bloodied hands of his friend
whose eyes are half-closed as if about to sleep
only they look down at what's left of his hands
that have been shot or smashed
with something heavy
the vigilantes carried
through the bent-up stalks
of surrounding fields,
come and gone like a storm.
Another man spreads his arms
as if welcoming someone home
from a long journey
except his eyes say that no one comes.
Around him black smoke curdles,
huge blossoms of smoke you feel
you could pluck from the air,
and around the last man too,
who holds a child over his head
like a sack of something he's lifted

from a truck and is about to throw into a pile
of more sacks and in the air
so many angels you can't breathe,
their wings in your face like fingers,
like a white-capped river of voices
the wind spits when whatever spirits survive
are called to cross over,
the howling blows rained down, rained down.

THE HAND THAT TAKES

Sometimes I think it's God I want,
that I need the holy spirit
as if the lost years,
the sins of my body and hands
could be forgiven.
The days not unlike a song
twist in my head
and something old and evil
clings like a bad smell
and a hand
wants to take and take.
Rain washes the blood
until the blood seeps away
but leaves a ruby
shadow on the ground.
Wings cut.
There was fire
in her eyes
so we didn't touch.
I wanted her silk
on my cock,
her lips, her nipples,
but soldiers ran wild
through Tet's streets

and spotlights
swung in arcs from jeeps.
You cannot hide
from what eats you.
She still calls me
from the room in an alley
where the boy I was
undressed
but kept one hand
on the black weapon
all through the night
of wronged love,
the worthless money
spread out on the bed
like a fan.
Yet tonight
through the years
I hear my woman speak
to our little boy
and the thousands
of holes in my brain
and their screaming
can't drown what sounds
like song to make him sleep,

like promises that are lies,
kisses that will not come
as he believes
forever to his lips.
I have grown up inside
a thing that I can't name.
I spoke with angels once.
Through their slipless
pastel dresses
I traced that ancient silhouette.
I imagined what I could do
to their bodies
but sharp wings
cut through their clothes
and their claws like a dog's
ripped a hole in the sky.
What used to save me
was my child's voice
singing at night in his bed
songs he'd learned at school
or the pills that gave me sleep
or the light come up
on rain-misted trees.
I have loved war.

I have loved the nights
of dragons and opium,
the wind from the river
in the angel's hair,
her skin like silk
on the balcony of the dead
in the blood
of my breaking free
because I did not die
with those who rose
beyond the green,
drowning like visions.
And after that dangerous love
no woman could save me
from the meaning of things.
I wanted to lie down with her
as if nothing had happened
and the air could be breathed
and the atoms of light
did not explode
in our faces like flares.
I heard a hallelujah
through the wind.
I heard a child's scream

and the rockets
crash through bamboo.
From the mother's legs
we are dropped into fire.
There is not even time
for the moon to turn away,
or the words to be said
and then mean nothing,
or the fear to make men
not kiss the dead.

THIS MAN

There's another world, in which this man
dragged his prize beagle pup
off the aqua deep-pile carpet
where it had shit and pissed in excitement
when the children had wrongly
carried it in to play.

He never broke his stride.
He grabbed the pearl-handled pistol from the closet
and he dragged that pup who whined
into the backyard of an evening
in an autumn stuck somewhere, lost
in the currents of larger, less important things.

IN THE AUTUMN VILLAGE

Half in the street and half
up on the sidewalk
in the Village off of Eighth
a man in the Saturday cold air
without shoes
tried to crawl across the street
through busy traffic.
I'm no better than you,
but you've got to help a man
who's trying to go someplace
on his hands and knees.
I don't know what it means to crawl,
or where you would go,
or in whose empty arms you could believe,

but I put my books down to help.
I offered my arm
as if to a girl
stepping from her father's porch
into an evening.
I thought he would pull himself
up on my arm
and walk away from us.

I was afraid, and bent over him
as if he might leap out at me.
I'm no goddamn better than you
but he couldn't move another inch
so I put my arms around him
and lifted him to the sidewalk.
The wind made some trees talk.
The city noise returned upon us,
a wave I could ride out on and away.

MAY

I wanted to stay with my dog
when they did her in
I told the young veterinarian
who wasn't surprised.
Shivering on the chrome table,
she did not raise her eyes to me when I came in.
Something was resolved in her.
Some darkness exchanged for the pain.
There were a few more words
about the size of her tumor and her age,
and how we wanted to stop her suffering,
or our own, or stop all suffering
from happening before us
and then the nurse shaved May's skinny leg
with those black clippers;
she passed the needle to the doctor
and for once I knew what to do
and held her head against mine.
I cleaved to that smell
and lied into her ear
that it would be all right.
The veterinarian, whom I'd fought
about when to do this thing
said through tears

that it would take only a few minutes
as if that were not a long time
but there was no cry or growl,
only the weight of her in my arms,
and then on the world.

THE CONFUSION OF PLANES
WE MUST WANDER IN SLEEP

I stood naked in the corner as my mother
changed the wet sheet and clucked her tongue though spoke
as kindly as she could, my father stirring angrily
in the bed across the hall. Lost, my legs sheened in piss,
I stumbled, drugged with the grief
children practice to survive. I was apart
from the cold and heavy smell. I was not attached
to the world though I followed my young and weary
mother into the timeless dark, and tonight

I pull my own son's blankets back and speak to him:
how nice a dry bed will be, how good to get up
without a fuss and go. I lift him to stand,
his penis a wand waving its way magically
before us, and something makes sense for once in my head,
the way that what we pass on is not always a gift,
not always grace or strength or music, but sometimes
a burden, and we have no choice but to live
as hard as we can inside the storm of our years
because even the weaknesses are a kind of beauty
for the way they bind us into what love, finally, must be.

THE BIOGRAPHY
OF FATTY'S BAR AND GRILLE

Liquor was involved,
hard drinking all through the afternoon
and longtime bad blood
like a sickness,
and a woman who had dyed her hair
black as asphalt and whose breasts
swung freely inside her printed dress.
The man with three fingers kept a pistol
in the silk inner pocket
of his sharkskin suit
and when the fat man
said one thing too many
to the woman under his breath
I heard that .22 pop three times
and watched the fat man
fall in a heap and grab his great belly.

Many people hit the floor,
though almost immediately
the shooter longed to bring the bullet back.
In disbelief he watched himself
convulse in fear and shame in the spidered mirror.
I remember how white his face became,

like a mask, like a spirit lost in its longing.
Then people began to rise up again.
Police and ambulance appeared.
The man with three fingers
was handcuffed with his arms before him
so when he smoked his cigarette
he looked like he was praying.

THE YEARS
WITHOUT UNDERSTANDING

My father did not read to me,
he would not quote anything or anyone,
he never alluded
as we are wont to say in my world
to poems or stories
to make a point or to teach me
some lesson about the life
beyond the slag heaps of our steel city
dying upon our dying lake.

And what you teach someone
with a belt across his back
is belts,
or I missed the point of those beatings
which were not so bad—
the loud voice in the hallway, then the belt
flashing
then the kisses on his lap.
If I could bring the words to you
as though from him,
clear as the air off this bay
you would see—

he is home from the foundry,
younger than I am now, the black
dust from the mill like a mask
and he is bending down to me
in the dusk where I've waited
on the steps of the bar
for his bus
and the cathedral
he makes with his fingers
opens to a silver dime
he twists before me
and lays down into my hands
for being good he says.

THE BLACK HOSE

A boy who knew enough to save for something
like the whim that took me downtown on the bus
one lost Saturday morning of my mother's birthday,
I sat in the back where the gasoline smell
made me dizzy and I closed my eyes but didn't
think of her, only of myself, basking in the light
and love that would fall down on me when I
handed her the box and she untied the bow to save
and lifted something shining out and held it up before us
like a promise taking shape for once in her hands,
though I didn't know what to buy, the bus door
hissing behind me because I'm in some kind of
state now, a trance that comes when you pull
at the cords of light that connect the mother to the boy,
the 1959 department store
opening up before me like a jeweled city.
In lingerie I found myself
surrounded by those torsos sheened in silk,
dreaming my mother, feeling the silk against me,
the two of us moving through a cloudy room
in a dance I can't remember until shame comes.
From out of nowhere the matron frowned,
asked what I wanted, hovered over me.

Confused and afraid I whispered, without thinking,
The black hose with rhinestones down the seams please
and pointed to the pair across the room
stretched over legs on the glass counter
as if about to step off
and I saw her in my mind slip them on,
her skirt hiked above the garters, the sun
catching in her tangled hair
until the matron made a sound in her throat
and looked at me with eyes that said
What's wrong with you dirty boy.

All the way home a sweet ache rocked me,
the silver package riding my lap
like a heavy wrong thing
I couldn't give up no matter how it
dragged me down to a place
where I could barely breathe or see or feel.
Whatever happened that spinning afternoon—
she ran her fingers over the rhinestone seams
or she didn't, she wore them out into an evening
or kept them forever in her drawer of impossible things—
doesn't matter. I would find my way into the light

of another woman into whose arms I fall
nights my fingers can't tear through the dark
that eats me, the silk stretched across her breasts,
the need for something womanly to raise me up
pounding in my head until I curl in sleep
away from those longings, ancient and blue.

BLUES AT THE EQUINOX

In the shadows
the woman dresses quietly,
beyond light the parking lot

spears through thin drapes,
her heart inclined
towards the miraculous.

What passes for love,
the miles and the years
and the rivers crossed no one could name,

what passes for love
is not always the fierce blessing
the mortal lovers give—and then grow pale—

but sometimes one heart robbing another
in a rented room, a great sadness
and a great happiness, at the same time, descending.

THE IMPOSSIBLE

Winter's last rain and a light I don't recognize
through the trees and I come back in my mind
to the man who made me suck his cock
when I was seven, in sunlight, between boxcars.
I thought I could leave him standing there
in the years, half smile on his lips,
small hands curled into small fists,
but after he finished, he held my hand in his
as if astonished, until the houses were visible
just beyond the railyard. He held my hand
but before that he slapped me hard on the face
when I would not open my mouth for him.

I do not want to say his whole hips
slammed into me, but they did, and a black wave
washed over my brain, changing me
so I could not move among my people in the old way.
On my way home I stopped in the churchyard
to try and find a way to stay alive.
In the branches a redwing flitted, warning me.
In the rectory, Father prepared
the body and blood for mass
but God could not save me from a mouthful of cum.

That afternoon some lives turned away from the light.
He taught me how to move my tongue around.
In his hands he held my head like a lover.
Say it clearly and you make it beautiful, no matter what.

THE FORMS
OF ELEVENTH AVENUE

I squatted like I'd learned in Dak To
on the seventh floor window ledge
across from the park of the homeless
contemplating the skyline and the loss.
In milky light behind me
the woman who would be exiled
slept, her feet moving
like a dog's in a dream.
Men smoked glass pipes
in the streetlight's
wash across the park.
Women tried to nurture
into existence
homes from cardboard boxes.
Four policemen talked
and snapped their sticks
on a park bench.
All night on the ledge
spirits called to me:
Come to us with your face
and your wings
they whispered
from their saintly streets

and the human things
could not save me.
Not the smell
of the woman's hair
in the morning
like street air after rain.
Not the corpses
waking in doorways.
Not the way everything changes,
continuously, like the sky.
What saved me
were the Latin prayers
come back from the years
like desire,
and the many mouths
open in absolution,
and the nakedness,
the belt flashing,
the fists from out of nowhere,
the abandonment of love.

from
SWEET LORAIN
(1996)

SITTING WITH THE BUDDHIST MONKS, HUE, 1967

Cool spring air through the window,
birds waking rain in the white
limbs of the shaken birch,
I remember
I was led through an ancient
musty maze of alleyways
and rooms where people looked up
from their cooking
and their endless ledgers
as if I were a mean and clumsy spirit
lost among them.

Into darkness I was delivered,
only candlelight
to show the heads bowed
to the clasped hands
rocking in prayer.

I thought he was taking me to his whore.
They did not teach us
the words for prayer or for peace.
I'd watched his hands
gesture in the half-lit alleyway

and his hands told me to follow,
his eyes asked me for money.

I have tried to let the green war go,
but those monks looked at me
across their circle of knowing
and my body somehow
rose off the floor.
their voices
ringing in my skull
like the cry of gut wound
in razor grass.

I was only a boy.
I didn't want to remember.
I wanted only the lily
to keep opening.

THE ONE

To the long mill's shadow
and stink we shared
with drunks who pissed
on the heater of our common
john
I go back.
To the bedroom I shared with my sister,
my bed squeezed
tight against the cool wall
so I could hold my body there
hot nights in the mill noise
until my legs stiffened
and I felt that hum.

In the corner of that room
waits the word
and the sound
of the belt.
My tall father
thin and muscled from mill work,
his hair black
thick and curly,
and his smile,
when he swung down on me,
I could not resist.

Through dark the belt
flashed across my back
though I knew he beat me
out of love
as when he finished
I knew to climb
inside the darkness of my own arms.
I knew the world
would stop spinning
uncontrollably
and the convulsions
stop rippling
and my mother
would come to touch me
with such care
as if I were teetering
at the edge of the abyss
and she would lead me
back into my life,
her fingers
whispering in my hair
that it would be all right,

and later still, after beer,
after the moon had risen
to its proper place
and the night
could allow some forgiveness,
he would call me into his lap,
and tell me I was the one.

WHAT I SAW AND DID IN THE ALLEY

Some lonely boy from the neighborhood
with the Saint Vitus' dance
from when a truck
backed over his wagon
nearly crushing his skull
made a crossbow
from the leaf-springs of a car
and haunted the summer dusk streets
beyond the long mill.

I found the cat
dead in the alley,
a homemade arrow
nicely through its skull.
Running home late,
I stumbled on the cat
and had to stop.
By the scruff of his alley neck
I held Mr. unknown cat
and looked into his eyes
green as new bamboo

and reckoned our kinship
of killing

in that alley and beyond
where needful of love and of blood
I had stunned the brown sparrow,
the robin and wren,
the wild canary in spring.
Don't ask how they felt
in my hands, still warm,
bubble of blood on their beaks;
to nowhere their dead wings unfold.

CARE

I didn't know what they wanted.
Six or seven
and in the care of two teenage
cousins drunk on beer
who dragged me through dark woods
behind their house.
I thought I saw black wings swoop down
to lift me, but no one came
so I followed them into a clearing
where they finished their beer
and loaded the rifle.
In the snow I was cold.
I watched them make a pyramid of cans
they blasted in turns with the rifle
so it sounded like someone's
bones being broken,
and then they looked at me.
They put a can in my hand
extended as far from my body
as all my strength allowed . . .

For a long time afterwards
I felt out of sync.
In school I would fall

into tunnels of snow
in my brain towards some center
until I heard my name
called from a great distance
and felt the teacher
shake my shoulders.
That night with my cousins
drunkenly loading their rifle,
I learned that fear has a shape
and a taste in your mouth
not like metal,
but more human and wrong.
I wanted to drop my arms and run away,
but they were wildly drunk
and stumbled in the frozen snow,
the rifle tangled between them
so I was afraid to move
until a shot caught the can in my hand
on its rim
so it vibrated through my fingers,
shook my brain and then exploded
into the moonlit snow behind me.
They laughed and slapped my back,

and just as thoughtlessly
as we had descended,
we rose again into the trees
towards the warm house
and its emerald
jungle of our lives.

AT THE CONFLUENCE OF MEMORY
AND DESIRE IN LORAIN, OHIO

Love could be a shape that unfolds
in rooms sullen and deformed by rain

Oh clothes torn off in that
frenzy

Oh seeing-eye
tongues

Oh saintly lies whispered
in evening's wrong light

Slam of hips
and her breasts would sway

I taste the bloody slit
in the night's cloth

THREE MEDITATIONS AT NGUYEN DU

i

I have loved more than a few good men
who were boys in the green
slanting rain of bullets
cut through yellow bamboo.

On the street of a thousand
sighs in Hanoi
I found a simple Buddha
high on a gold lacquered shelf
in a small room of the honored dead.

Pulled down to my knees
by a girl in a yellow ao dai,
I was no longer afraid
of the spirit I was
trying to become the man.

ii

Before me, my father's
immigrant father
appeared in rosy incense smoke.

He who had made shoes from sheets of hard leather
with his hands and a knife.

He who had fixed all broken things
and butchered lambs in spring.
He who in his anger
had made my father kneel on dry corn
his raging hands had shucked
across the bathroom floor.

iii

I have never knelt on dry corn,
the way my father
has never prayed
on the floor of a stranger's
house in Hanoi,

yet through the years
that cling
to the razor sharp kernels

came the belt
and the backhands
out of nowhere, my father,
beating like an angel
for heaven, through me.

THAT FINISHED FEELING

Wrong words brought them together
     outside the steel mill
bar of tired, nervous men,

wrong words to the wrong man,
     wrong street, wrong night
the blood so near their skin

that this man full of iron ingot's
     heat, and this other good man
in their rage

crossed a line
     which in the August
night is pure

so they face off,
     and in our muted needs
we circle their sweat-shined

muscle and bone
     twisted in the light
of the night shift cranes

beating beating
      Oh say can you see
these strong and grown men

whose lives are too heavy
      to bear the bloody other
stranger into another day.

HYMN OF MY REPUBLIC

Summer of my dumb awakening,
nineteen fifty-six, a solitary

neighbor man who walked every day to the mill
through south Lorain with a gimpy stride

and lived alone above the bar of our fathers
emerged into light

and passed around among us boys
who chanced to be nearby

and not afraid
some cool gear

from his war,
number WW II.

I got the leather pilot's hat, oh Lord.
I put it on

and nothing could touch me
wandering long into the dusk,

hymn of my republic
on my lips, my rough spirit

raised up somehow into glory, that boy's
grave initiative,

that blood
spilled first in the roses.

OUR 17TH STREET YEARS

Just the luck of the draw

my father would say

slouched in his white T-shirt

longneck bottle of beer

dangling from his terrible hand

He'd meant to tell me what the world was

so I imagined

a life of my hand held out

the good spirits waiting somehow

in the misty bamboo groves   yet

no words came as I had hoped

no webs of light connecting me

no paths that said to follow

no dove against the sky   no sky

CARP

We fished for carp whose flesh would never find
our lips, the bottom feeders fathers said to kill.
We fished at night with bloody bait designed
to draw them up from river mud. Our will
was to possess a life not ours, to make
those glowing spirit bodies understand
our need for blood spilled simply for the sake
of what we thought it took to be a man.
I'll never understand that rage we knew,
that knife that someone gouged into the eyes
of carp we caught but didn't think to do
the killing right, and wasted lives despised
for reasons lost now in the blur of days.
Not boys, but something darker, something crazed.

CONVERSATION OF OUR BLOOD

That his father brought the butcher up
to tattoo a watch in indigo
on my grandfather's wrist
with the time his steerage
would unbound its lines
and sail,
not for a new world,
just a different one,
is as true as this sky I could love.
But please, only you
of continents abandoned
pass judgment,
only you of quarantine
and the various cleansings
and the dialects
impossible to understand.

His mother wrapped some bread up
in a white square of light
and from their stone house on the hill
they must have walked
north to the station
across the pasture
and followed the tracks

in what must have seemed
a moment outside the world,
the gray dawn coming down
on their sweet and level plain.
From the station they traveled
farther north
in a crowded common car
that must have lulled them to the harbor
and the great pushing
mass of men like him,
and their women
dragging children through the mud
and the green confusion,
his father not stopping
to wave from the dock,
his wrist burning the blue time.

By the fish smell and oil drum din
he bedded down
something in my chest tells me.
With his blanket
I imagine him mark out his place.
I rub my face
to try and find

the shape of his jaw
and I do, and his love for the good drink
which is never the last,
and the startled look of surprise
always in our eyes
and the pull of him,
like a wire, in my heart.

The years that I didn't know mattered
must have been those
black wings that passed through us
and were gone.
I finally took the slow,
heaving ferry out
to where you waited
your long Ellis Island hours.
I tried to find a column
you would have leaned against,
a window out of which
you would have seen your world
taking shape
across the river we stole, Grandfather,
as we stole all of our rivers.

THREE FISH

Duc Thanh brought me three fish
      he had caught in the small lake on Nguyen Du.

They were the color of pearls;
      they were delicate and thin. Already

winter was in the wind from China,
      voices of ancestors on swan's wings.

This late in the season,
      evening traffic's hum and weave beginning to rise

beyond the guardians of the gate,
      these fish are a great gift.

I was in my room,
      lost in a foreign silence.

I wanted to eat the miles up somehow,
      I wanted to split my soul in two

so I could stay forever
      in the musty guest house pleasures.

I was that far away, that lost
        when he called to me, ghost that he is,

across the courtyard, and in moonlight,
        held up three silver fish.

OUR MIDDLE YEARS

Because in our middle years
        we had grown contemplative,
we asked out loud for the fire;

we had grown mostly cautious too,
        except in matters of the flesh
between the thighs.

We were waiting out the end of the century
        and wondered where the fire had gone,
night sky

empty as a skirt
        except for the wing bone noise
of the night hawk

diving for insects
        with a more than abundant precision
required by our times.

ELEGY FOR PETER

That night we drank warm whiskey
in our parked car
beyond woods now lost to the suburbs,
I fell in love with you.

What waited was the war
like a bloody curtain,
and a righteous moment
when the lovely boy's

spine was snapped,
then the long falling into hell.
But lately, you've been calling me
back through the years of bitter silence

to tell me of another river of blood
and of the highland's
howl at dusk of human voices
blasted into ecstasy.

That night in sweet Lorain
we drank so long and hard
we raised ourselves
above the broken places,

mill fires burning
red against the sky. Why
is there is no end
to this unraveling.

MY EARLY TRAINING

On the banks of West Lake near Hanoi
      the Abbot stepped from shadows
at Tran Quoc Pagoda. Wind

lifted lotus blossoms;
      spirits released themselves
from banyan roots old as Christ.

The holy man pointed my way
      towards two skinny dogs
playing like children in the perfumed garden

and then to the Buddha, high on an altar
      beyond the dusty, sun-reeked
courtyard of my imaginings, a lesson

I still struggle to understand.
      And oh the days and ways of woe since then,
this moon who won't love us

as we need, only the unrequited touch,
      only the empty skin on skin of stolen hours
fractured out of time

and these sharp wings that beat
        through black, star-shredded space
vast as memory, but not everlasting.

MEDITATION AT MELVILLE AVE.

I'd fallen asleep
on the white wicker chair
on the back porch,
the green yard and garden
so lush it seemed almost
as if the hot, troubled city
was not pressing in
against every inch of air.
Hot for so early in June
yet a breeze came now and then
to shake the live oak's branches
and turn the maple's leaves
up as if a storm were near.
I'd fallen asleep and dreamed
I was someone else,
someone wholly unburdened
and with hope.
I had been briefly among friends
who had gone away to a wedding
of other friends
who were also strangers,
only the green war between us,
only the sandalwood smell in her hair.

Half in and out of sleep
I heard two sets of chimes
in wind that came and went
and seemed to play a song
that rose and fell,
some form my body knew.
Beyond the yard,
sirens played out their flat complaint.
Trouble. He got drunk.
She spit in his face.
He lashed out at her.
If you think there's no blood
in the streets
then you live in a dream.
The chimes rose and fell
and rose and fell again.
The friends stay and stay.
The witnesses of evening
all settle into the cacophony
of familiar fears.
The silver leaves turn up
but no storm comes.

MEDITATION AT HUE

Some nights I still fear the dark among trees,
those last few ambush hours before morning.

I fear the jungle of a thousand sighs
which calls and calls to me.

I don't care I have to tell you
about the angels who fell

dead from gunships into the valley of tears.
I don't care if I keep you from the wedding wine.

Priests blessed weapons in the mist of Ca Lu.
I want to die in the mango groves

of this green river valley,
children dancing after my corpse.

ON THE AMBIGUITY OF
INJURY AND PAIN

When I saw the X ray of my boy's broken bones
the young doctor held up to the light,
a fist closed around my heart.
Behind us in the gurney
he was lost in his pain,
betrayed by the world
like birds by false spring.
The little Mozart piece would be abandoned
to summer evenings jangled out of time,

and back at school
his classmates rush to him
in wonder at his wound
and scratch their names into the plaster.
And tonight, when I bathe him he is shy.
When I try to run the soap
and rag between his legs
he stops me with his free hand
the way I've been stopped by women.
We move in the old way, around each other.
Kisses so sweet. Dark room of joy.

RED SQUIRREL

I think it's fine the squirrel lives with us,
in secret in our fifties-style ranch
beneath the pale, unsheltered sky.
From the world she is a gift of sorts,
a strange and awkward blessing
who wakes us from our cold dawn sleep

to watch the sun come up through trees.
I think it means the air in here must be alive;
the stale basement walls a womb,
a nest inside a womb beyond
the muted rise and fall, our voices
as we move from room to room.

And she must know the odd forgiven terrors
of the family life, the love that has to fight
to stay alive. So from this man at my front door
I turn away, his traps and poison
held before him like a gift, a gilded
reckless sin I know for once not to embrace.

WORDS LIKE COLD WHISKEY
BETWEEN US AND PAIN

I no longer covet the stranger's wife.
He had opened his house to me

one night when I didn't know
what world I was in.

We had only the green war in common,
the Jacob's ladder to climb.

We were deep in the country,
evening coming down like a gate,

all the good creatures stirred into song
when she came outside after dishes

and stood in the backdrop kitchen light,
her hair matted black at her temples

and her eyes
lit in the satisfaction

of good work done
and in my mind I wanted her,

my face a shameless
mask in the dark.

I thought I could smell the river.
I thought I could hear its rush.

Stars began to beat down on us.
It doesn't mean anything. Here, I let you go.

BEAR MEADOW

In this field of day lilies
just opening, beating for sun
in this lush summer bear meadow,
I tried to find a way
to stay in your world, wife.
The field hummed with life,
the bugs and frogs
and jeering birds
but no words came
as I had hoped
from the sky
blue as a marble.
I tried to lose my self
in the woods of beyond
but only paths fell under my feet
and I glimpsed the shape
that nature is
unfolding in the roots
and limbs connecting us
with threads of light
but then so quickly gone.
I could imagine
an emptiness without you,

without your face in my hands
like a flower
I could imagine something
bottomless and cold.
We have traveled
deep into the center
of something we can't name
yet stayed side by side
when the light died
and the road ground down
to a cutback through trees
and there was nowhere to run.
What I have to give you
I feel in my blood,
many small fires
burning into one.

FEVER DREAM IN HANOI

The gold red and green carp
surfaces in the lake where I struggle.
Angry and impatient with me
he shakes his head
big as a baby's head
towards the lake's center.
I'd been half-swimming,
half-treading water
to try to make the shore
where small lights
blinked around the perimeter
beside tiny stands
where women squat
in that particular
Vietnamese way
selling their few packs of cigarettes,
their few bottles of warm beer.

Lovers linger too,
among banyan trees tangled.
They nuzzle each other.
They coo and laugh
for the minutes stolen
from the crowded family houses,

and all seem to call to me
when I wake in the lake
of the returned sword
to the carp who shakes his head
towards the shrine on the island
lit only with light
of the Buddha's eyes.

I thought my life was calling
from the lamp-lit lovers' shore.
I thought my death called too
from the dark water, deeper,
but the carp shakes his head,
old hooks and fishing line
strung in the moon like a beard.
He swishes the fan of his tail
and I'm on my back,
floating somehow towards the temple,
face of the carp
changed, a human smile
on his lips, the moon
slashed across the blood-gills' pulse.
The lovers turn away from each other
to the lake's black edge,

and the old women
blow out their small lanterns
and turn too towards the lake.
I'm being towed now,
the gold carp's hooks
snagged through the skin on my back.
With his eyes he tells me
not to fight.
He tells me of my perfect death
waiting at the shrine
and then I wake,
burning with fever
in the guest house on Nguyen Du
by the lake where lovers
walk in the dark
evening's desire.
Two men and a boy

hold coal-hot doss sticks
to points on my wrists and feet
where my cold blood is still.
Another man taps needles
deep into my back
down my spine

until a cry or grunt
escapes my lips
and he nods
his happy affirmation
as my gut begins to stir,
a snake coming alive,
uncurling itself inside me,
my head swimming,
my skin hot then cold
then hot again,
musty waves of sickness
through which he tows me
with his needles
and I float.
I let go of everything.
I let go my family
the thousands of miles away.
I let go my days
and my hours
and my sad minutes
and I let go the love.
I let go the words.
Every word ever uttered.
I let go the world.

I spin off the world,
hooks in my back
pulling me upwards, upwards and away.

AFTER THE OTHERS

     everything changed.
They took the mountains
     then crossed the river
swiftly in their long boats.
     Always they have come.
They took the trees.
     They took the brown earth

     and the small houses.
They silenced the voices
     and took the words
so no one could tell the story
     of the time before
because they have always come,
     because there is no time before.

     Under a single blue cloud
a man and a woman touched each other.
     An unfaithful gratuity of dogs appeared.
The old people stopped speaking.
     They would not bear witness
to the visitations
     or to the jangled, rising noise of gabble

conjured in place of a history. God
was invented
    so they could bear their suffering.
In the end
    they had only each other
and wandering, alone,
    that was not enough.

THE HAPPY LAND

I dread those lace doilies
      lonely women stitch
for the ill,

and the surplice of the unchaste
      boy who serves the morning mass,
though always

I have believed and practiced prayer,
      even when I stalked those alleys
to murder in mindless boyhood boredom

so many righteous songbirds
      that I will never know their forgiveness
which I had imagined

would feel like their tiny hearts felt
      sputtering out in my hand because
I had launched those jagged stones so precisely.

PRAISE WOUND DIRT SKIN SKY

Praise wound.
Praise dirt in the wound
that made the metal
fester in the skin.
Praise wound
that closed over
like night sky.
Praise the sharp
cutting metal
exploded into splinters,
physics of shrapnel,
my science.
Praise skin,
how it pushed
the splinters out
against all odds
through the scar
to the cot
in the city
where I waited
where I walked
in the place of emperors.

THE INEXPLICABLE ABANDONMENT
OF HABIT IN ECLIPSE

My father and his father
punched the card in and out every day
and did not love their lives.
They worked too hard for nothing wages,

then bitched to their wives in restless beds
and grew around themselves
a coat of sullenness.
I was not conscience-calmed then.

Almost always I played a silent war game to myself,
yet a memory of my father
leaning in the doorway
watching night birds

sweep and then
pass upwards
into a suddenly dark afternoon sky
gives me no peace.

ELEGY FOR HER WHOSE NAME
YOU DON'T KNOW

She only felt your heart
beat on her sex is all, but still
you can't bear how alone we are,
so before the nothing,
on the lotus path,
you pause to consider
what light you would stand in
for the thousand lives.

We learn this by letting go. We learn this
from moonlight fallen wild on the still pond.
In the grass of her grave you find sense.
In the green grass,
grown to the shape of her body.

RIVER JOURNAL

I keep a wall of rock or trees
        to my back. My eyes will always find a way
that's safe

because I've always feared what's underneath things.
        Naked river. Devout river.
Implacable river that touches itself.

I wanted to stand in the river one late evening
        storm. Some of the spirits told me   Go back.
Some of the spirits called me

to their company in deep water.
        Dark living shapes slid past, wind
too warm for the hour.

Such a soaking rain this evening, lord.
        All the little cities I'd held in my hands,
washed away.

ANNIVERSARY OF MYSELF

A lifetime ago

I squatted down on a curb
in a frozen twilight parking lot

some fucking where

and looked up into the near
apartment's windows
and at the lives going on
behind them in the light.

The fingers of my gloves had holes.
I don't know what I was doing.
There had been a war
and my people
had grown disenchanted.

I had a fifth of somebody's
whiskey in my pocket. That night
the liquor kept me warm. Now
I flitter branch to branch outside your window,
lit with a thousand watts of something
I can taste and feel but cannot see.

I am moth wing in summer sky,
night bird not blinded or butchered
by your unkempt, sleepless dogs.

WHY I'M NOT AFRAID

To be afraid of the wrong and of the cruel
      is to make them more real than they are.
What the takers want to take they can have.

They can have the name
      and they can have the face.
They can have the cheap suit

and the sweet wine.
      They can have the lawn and the garden
furniture. They can have the future

where they must smuggle
      their tiny selves of a self
into the lives of others

to have any life at all. I won't
      let them have the words.
They cannot take the words

or their seamless music,
      and with no false tears
can they bless or curse words

into stubborn human shapes
      against the corruption
of their minds and of their historic elms.

The tunnels of goodness
      that we may pass through
they make thick and grim

with the weight of their bodies;
      flesh that isn't flesh,
blood that doesn't know

the river's name.
      They can have the flesh.
They can have the hands

and their rings.
      They can have the offices
of the nothing that they inhabit

like the newly dead.
      They can have the history
that will not

remember for them
      what grace may do
for the sharp

and for the flicking tongue.
      They can have the tongue.
They can have the lips

I know they have watched
      across the room
in their spiteful reckless

longing for the light inside of us.
      They can have the light.
They can have the chill

and the silence of their
      own pale shadows
that won't work anymore.

AND WE CAME HOME

to the bloody village,
to whole streets of loss,
whole rooms,
and sat up all the first night

saying what passed for prayer
because we did not know
how to live in the new world,
and I would take you,

who are my rose inside me
blossoming,
to where the sidewalks are so wide for promenade,
what the French abandoned,

like their mistresses
and their architecture
haunted by the savage rule of class, gentlemen
who'd hanged their brothers in the doorways of another time.

We could walk down Nguyen Du Street
beside the lake,
then follow the lost trolley tracks
back to old Hanoi

and find the seven ancient gates
to save at least their memory. No one
understands how we felt.
Kill it all. Kill it all.

THE CHOOSING OF MOZART'S
FANTASIE OVER SUICIDE

The great music I watched
    find its way
through a broken boy's world
    of walls and walls.
I swear to Christ

I never knew for sure if this could be. We say
    We tried it all but nothing works,
not even when you give
    your heart held out in open hands. We say
We almost lost him once or twice,

yet never did we cleave that way before.
    And he cleaved too.
He loved the music deep somewhere inside himself
    and found the peaceful thing
the sometimes mad man left behind

between the ache of melody
    and melody undone, and brave
he let himself come back to us
    and never mind that other boy
he'd thought he had to be.

PINEAPPLE

In the white light midnight Stop & Shop
        a woman asked me
how to choose the pineapple

best for eating right away, that night.
        She said she liked to suck
the juice; her lips were full

and puckered into smile.
        She held one in her hands
like the head of a garroted man

and squeezed with her thumbs
        where the eyes would be.
Towards me

she thrust the syrup prickly leaves
        until they twitched just inches from my face.
I lied and said I didn't know.

Some black hair fell across her face;
        her eyes so comely
for the simple moment's needs,

her shirt unbuttoned low
           so I could see
the slope of breasts

she wanted me to see
           when she bowed her pineapple bow.
I smelled another world on her,

that scent I'd want to breathe and eat too much
           the way we do. I walked away.
I lied and said I didn't know.

THE NOTHING REDEMPTION

Some men's voices rose and fell far away.
        Time changed. Time got
stupid and I stood in line with the gobs,
        our drawers at our feet
so our cheeks we could pull apart.

One boy's
        hole was plastered
closed with his own dried months of shit,
        and the doctor
called a second doctor in

and the sergeants arrived feigning aimlessness.
        Oh la the boy sang
to the doctors who giggled
        like men when they dream about war.
I could not imagine

that a man would shit himself
        and let his own shit
dry himself closed.
        I didn't know that you could do that
so they would not take you

into the state;
        so they would not make you
cross through that door of lies
        into the greenery's mist.
All night that night I rode out

on a slow train with my cousin,
        and drunk, I pissed
from the upper berth
        down onto him
passed out in the berth below.

He never woke up
        but I thought I should wash him
soapy clean for the killing
        that I didn't know waited
for us like a bloody

handkerchief,
        snagged in the bushes,
found by the beast
        who joins in the search
for the slaughtered.

THE SINGING AND THE DANCING

I found a hole in the stall in the public toilet
    at the university where I work. Four inches across,

the sharp metal
    looked like it had been torn and peeled back in a rage.

From where I sat to do my chore
    the hole was almost level with my eyes.

For looking in? Out? Like you
    I have a greater need for love

of any kind,
    so I imagined the man

cutting and tearing
    and bending back

the metal toilet wall
    to make a human hole,

and I almost see the penis come,
    a shy and hungry thing.

In what looks like a rage,
      a hole was torn into the wall

between toilets
      so men could do

a kind of loving
      on this river of two minds.

OUR INDEPENDENCE DAY

I didn't know our night
trees could feel this safe,
three a.m., an early dove

coos for someone;
stars and more stars.
I didn't know

what I didn't know.
I didn't want
a life of anything then, only

a life.
Someone told me
Let it go, boy,

let the green
untangle from your body . . .
We used to say

It don't mean nothing
over bodies we'd find in muddy battle.
We used to say

God and Mummy in our half sleep
between red glare
rockets roaring in. Here,

the night trees feel safe;
at least no human beings
luminous in the sultry garden.

THE FUTURE

At last there are too many histories,
        so the day-lilies'
unforgiving of late spring

means only
        that the cold
snapped some buds in the night

and has nothing to do
        with our little lives.
We have come to worship the word

for its measure and for its commerce
        and so we have forgotten
much that we had learned

in the old way of reckless
        flight and woeful prayer,
and we have lost

our wild need to make believe.
        But in our denials, exquisitely,
we are accomplished,

and we have learned
    how to teach this to others. Yet tonight
I almost feel in my brain

this summer's soaking rain
    all through these late flowers
as if they were growing inside of me,

a thing we could not account for, here.
    We would say
It's only rain in the world

and not in your heart,
    only flowers of our given names
who have no use for us.

THE HAPPINESS OF OTHERS

is not like the music I hear
    after sex
with my wife of the decades

my wife
    of the ocean night grass
my wife

of the milk heavy mother breasts
    drowsily dipping towards me
my wife my rope my bread

OUR LIES AND THEIR BEAUTY

I have loved most
        the incongruous,
the wildly pointless,

the oddly non-self
        aggrandizing;
how one sweet man

whose mouth I would still kiss,
        lied to me
that his ne'er-do-well father

stood once,
        alone out on a thin steel beam
dangled

twenty stories
        above the teeming city
by a nervous crane.

The man that he lied was his father
        wears a white muscle t-shirt
in the photograph;

his black hair is curly
          and tangled
nicely in that high city wind.

His legs spread like a dog's,
          his fists
poised on his defiant hips,

he smiles a fearlessness
          that you want to but
can't quite believe.

One sad night,
          my friend showed me
a bent-up photograph

of this man on a beam,
          and I did not tell him
how I'd seen it on postcards

many times before.
          It could have been his father.
They were just then building the Waldorf.

My friend lied
        because he wanted his father
to be the man up there in his lie,

and because he wanted to weave something
        frightened that he saw inside of me
with something

that he saw inside of himself,
        the beauty
that must never always be the lie.

NOTES

Executioner:

The epigram "Something goes through the world/Without speaking to anyone" is from Charles Simic's poem "White."

The passage "Out of the horror there rises a musical ache that is beautiful" is from a letter to the author from James Wright, written kindly in response to some early poems about the author's experience in the American War in Vietnam.

The epigram "There was no light; there/was no light at all . . ." for the poem "Him, on the Bicycle" is from a poem by Theodore Roethke.

The book is dedicated to Charles Simic.

A Sack Full of Old Quarrels:

This book is dedicated to my mother and father.

A Romance:

The epigram "It still has not been born,/it is both music and the word/and therefore of all living things/the indestructible connection" is from a poem by Osip Mandelstam.

The final two italicized lines of "I Have Had My Time Rising and Singing" are from James Agee's *A Death in the Family*.

This book was dedicated to Jean and to Anna Grasa.

The Monkey Wars:

This book is dedicated to Cheryl Flowers.

Song of Napalm:

The lines "My home, my country,/the heart split in two . . ." which serve as an epigram for this book were spoken to me by Miss Tao as she showed me a mock tiger cage in Ho Chi Minh City in 1986, very much like the real tiger cage where she had been imprisoned by the then South Vietnamese government for her antiwar activities as a sixteen-year-old schoolgirl in Ho Chi Minh City in 1968.

The lines "What did I know, what did I know/of love's austere and lonely offices?" which serve as an epigram for Part II of this book are from Robert Hayden's poem "Those Winter Sundays."

This book is dedicated to Miss Tao and to Reg Gibbons.

What Saves Us:

The title poem is for Sally.

218

"They Name Heaven" was written in memory of Tomas Rivera.

"The Sky in Daduza Township" is based on a photograph by Paul Weinberg (Afrapix), which appeared originally in *Tri-Quarterly # 69* (Spring/Summer 1987). The poem is dedicated to Reg Gibbons.

The title "The Hand That Takes" is inspired by Laurie Anderson's song "O Superman."

The lines " . . . is not always the fierce blessing/the mortal lovers give—and then grow pale—" from "Blues at the Equinox" are a variation on lines from John Keats.

"The Impossible" is for Toby Thompson.

This book is dedicated to JKW.

Sweet Lorain:

The lines "¡Con la belleza no se come!/¿Qué piensas que en la vida?" (You cannot eat the beauty/What do you think life is?) are from Angel Gonzalez, *Astonishing World*, translated by Steven Ford Brown and Gutierrez Revuelta (Milkweed, 1993).

"Conversation of Our Blood" is in memory of Ivan Grasa, 1896–1975.

"Three Fish" is in memory of Ngo Vinh Vien.

"Elegy for Peter" is in memory of Peter Shagovac, killed outside Da Nang, 1967.

"Meditation at Melville Ave." is for Leslie and Kevin.

"On the Ambiguity of Injury and Pain" is for Andrew Weigl.

"Red Squirrel" is for Dave Smith.

"Bear Meadow" is for JKW, written on the occasion of our twentieth wedding anniversary.

"Fever Dream in Hanoi" is for BH.

New Poems 1995–1998:

For the poem "After the Others" I have shamelessly paraphrased passages from Milton's "Paradise Lost," especially from Book XII. (Writing a poem while visiting the tomb of Burns, Keats wrote, "I sin against thy native skies.")

"Why I'm Not Afraid" is for Tim, where I learned the story.

"Our Independence Day" was inspired by a conversation with and is dedicated to Charlie Simic.

"Our Lies and Their Beauty" is for Duke, with gratitude for his exquisite lies.

220

BRUCE WEIGL was born in Lorain, Ohio in 1949. He is the author of ten collections of poetry, most recently *Song of Napalm*, (Atlantic Monthly Press, 1988), *What Saves Us* (TriQuarterly Books, 1992) and *Sweet Lorain* (TriQuarterly Books, 1996). Weigl is also the editor or coeditor of three collections of critical essays, most recently *Charles Simic: Essays On The Poetry* (University of Michigan Press, 1996), as well as an anthology of poetry, fiction and nonfiction: *Between The Lines: Writings on War and its Social Consequences*, (coedited with Kevin Bowen. University of Massachusetts Press, 1996). In addition Weigl has published three volumes of poetry in translation: *Poems from Captured Documents*, co-translated from the Vietnamese with Nguyen Thanh (University of Massachusetts Press, 1994), *Mountain River: Poetry from the Viet Nam Wars*, coedited and co-translated from the Vietnamese with Nguyen Ba Chung and Kevin Bowen (University of Massachusetts Press, 1998), and *Angel Riding A Beast*, poems by Liliana Ursu, co-translated from the Romanian with the author (Northwestern University Press, 1998).

Weigl's poetry, translations, essays, articles, reviews, and interviews have appeared in such magazines as *The Nation*, *TriQuarterly*, *Field*, *The Kenyon Review*, *The New Yorker*, *The New York Times*, *Western Humanities Review*, *American Poetry Review*, *The Southern Review*, *Ploughshares*, *Paris Review*, *Antaeus*, and *Harper's*. In addition, his poems have been widely

221

anthologized, most recently in *The Best American Poetry, 1994*, edited by A. R. Ammons and David Lehman, *The Morrow Anthology of Younger American Poets, Poets of the '90's*, Paul Fussell's *Anthology of Modern War Literature*, and in *Against Forgetting: 20th-Century Poetry of Witness*, edited by Carolyn Forche. Weigl's poetry has been translated into Vietnamese, Chinese, Czech, German, Dutch, Spanish, Bulgarian, Romanian and Slovenian, and published internationally. For his work Weigl has been awarded a Patterson Poetry Prize, the Pushcart Prize twice, a prize from the Academy of American Poets, "The Breadloaf Fellowship in Poetry," a YADDO Foundation Fellowship and a National Endowment for the Arts Grant for poetry. He is past president of the Associated Writing Programs.